Snap books™ Crafts

Beginning Knitting

Stitches with Style

by Kay Melchisedech Olson

Capstone press®

Mankato, Minnesota

Snap Books are published by Capstone Press,
151 Good Counsel Drive, P.O. Box 669, Mankato, Minnesota 56002.
www.capstonepress.com

Library of Congress Cataloging-in-Publication Data
Olson, Kay Melchisedech.
    Beginning knitting : stitches with style / by Kay Melchisedech Olson.
    p. cm.—(Snap books. Crafts)
    Summary: "A do-it-yourself crafts book for children and pre-teens
on beginning knitting"—Provided by publisher.
    Includes bibliographical references and index.
    ISBN-13: 978-0-7368-6473-2 (hardcover)
    ISBN-10: 0-7368-6473-3 (hardcover)
    1. Knitting—Juvenile literature. 2. Knitting—Patterns—
Juvenile literature. I. Title. II. Series.
TT820.O42 2007
746.43'2—dc22   2006004101

Editor: Megan Schoeneberger
Designer: Bobbi J. Wyss
Production Artist: Renée T. Doyle
Illustrator: Kate Opseth
Photo Researcher: Kelly Garvin

Photo Credits:
Brand X Pictures/Nicole Katano, 25 (top); Capstone Press/Karon Dubke, cover (all), 4 (top), 5 (all), 6 (all), 9, 10, 11 (all),
12, 13, 15, 16, 17 (all), 18, 19, 20–21 (belt), 21 (girl), 22, 23 (all), 24 (all), 25 (bottom), 26–27, 28 (left), 29 (left), 32;
Shutterstock/Simone van den Berg, 4 (bottom)

The author wishes to thank her grandmother, Myrtle Born, for teaching her how to knit so many years ago.
Her patience and encouragement helped to develop a skill that has been enjoyed for a lifetime.

Go Metric!

It's easy to change measurements to metric! Just use this chart.

To change	into	multiply by
inches	centimeters	2.54
inches	millimeters	25.4
feet	meters	.305
yards	meters	.914
ounces (liquid)	milliliters	29.57
ounces (liquid)	liters	.029
cups (liquid)	liters	.237
pints	liters	.473
quarts	liters	.946
gallons	liters	3.78
ounces (dry)	grams	28.35
pounds	grams	453.59

Table of Contents

CHAPTER 1

Just Knit It

Stop dreaming about learning to knit. Start doing it.

If you think knitting is too complicated, think again. It's simply a matter of looping yarn over and over. Believe it or not, you only need to learn two stitches—the knit stitch and the **purl** stitch. All knitting is just a combination of those two stitches. They may seem a little tricky at first, but don't get discouraged. The simple projects in this book are perfect for beginners.

Fingering weight

Worsted weight

Bulky (chunky) weight

Weighty Issues

The "weight" of yarn refers to how thick the strand is. Very fine yarn is called "fingering" yarn. Very thick yarn is called "bulky" or "chunky." Medium-thick yarn is usually called "worsted weight."

Need Needles?

Knitting needles come in different sizes. The smaller the number, the smaller the needle. We've suggested needle sizes for each project. Use whatever needle you've got that is close to the size listed.

CHAPTER 2

Get Going!

Okay, you're ready to go. What do you need?

All you need are knitting needles, yarn, and determination. It also helps to know someone who knits. She can help you out if you get stuck. She may also be able to lend you a pair of needles and some leftover yarn.

Before you can begin, you have to know how to **cast on** stitches. Once you have the stitches on the needle, you add rows of stitches. When you're finished, you **bind off** the stitches to get the project off the needle without coming apart.

Casting On

For this way of casting on, you need only one of your needles. Start by tying a slipknot about 15 inches from the end of the yarn. Slip your needle into the loop. The knot is now your first stitch. The next steps will show you how to add more stitches.

1 Hold needle in your right hand, letting both strands of yarn hang. Put your left index finger and thumb between the two strands and spread them apart.

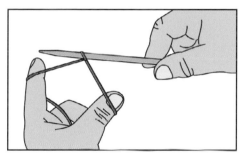

2 Slip needle under the loop around the thumb.

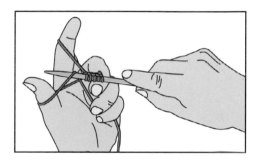

3 Bring needle up and under the loop on the forefinger from behind. Swing needle back through the loop on the thumb.

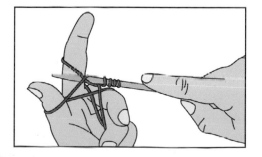

4 Carefully slip your thumb out of the loop. A very loose stitch is now on the needle.

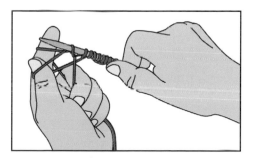

5 Tighten the stitch onto the needle as shown. Repeat until the number of loops on your needle equals how many stitches you want per row.

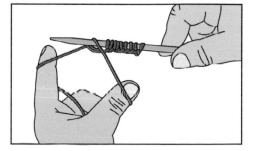

Knit Stitch

Now what? Take a deep breath, because it's time to try the knit stitch. Hold the knitting needle with the cast-on stitches in your left hand and the empty needle in your right. Now go for it!

1 Slip the right needle into the first stitch on the left needle as shown. The right needle should be under the left.

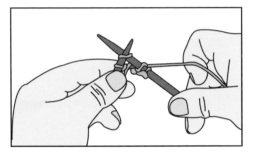

2 With your right hand, bring the yarn up and around the front of the right needle as shown.

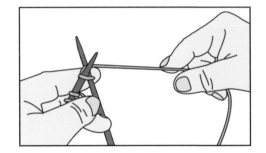

3 Catch the yarn strand with the tip of the right needle and pull it down through the same first stitch.

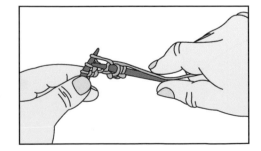

4 Slide the left needle out of the new stitch, which is now formed on the right needle.

5 Repeat for the desired number of stitches. At the end of the row, all the stitches will be on your right needle. Turn the right needle around and hold it in your left hand. Then put the empty needle in your right hand and start the next row.

Binding Off

After you finish your last row, bind off to make sure your project doesn't come apart.

1 Knit two stitches onto the right needle. Insert left needle under the first stitch.

2 With the left needle, slip the first stitch over the second. Knit one more stitch onto the right needle.

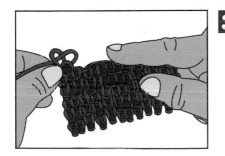

3 Repeat step 2 until one stitch remains. Cut the yarn and bring it through the final stitch.

Finish with Fringe

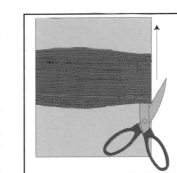

1 Loosely wind yarn around a piece of cardboard. Cut across one end.

2 With a crochet hook, draw folded end of yarn through a space or stitch at the bottom edge of your work.

3 Use a crochet hook to pull loose yarn ends through the loop of folded yarn. Pull loose yarn ends tight.

CHAPTER 3

Squares Are Cool

You can make so many things from knitted squares.

Got that knit stitch figured out? Just keep knitting rows until the piece is as long as it is wide. Bind off the stitches and you've got a cool knitted square.

A dishcloth is a great first project. It's square, so you don't need to follow a pattern. And don't worry if you **drop a stitch** and have a hole in your work. The dishes certainly won't mind.

Here's what you need

* knitting needles (medium size, such as 5, 6, or 7)
* cotton yarn (Cotton is best because it can really soak up water.)
* scissors
* yarn needle

Here's what you do

1 Cast on about 20 stitches (more or less, depending on how big you want your dishcloth to be).

2 Knit the same number of stitches in every row.

3 Continue until your work is as long as it is wide. (Tip: No need to measure. Take the bottom right corner of the work and fold it up to the stitches on the needle. When it forms a perfect triangle, you've got a perfect square.)

4 Bind off stitches.

5 With yarn needle, weave in yarn tails. Trim tail ends with scissors.

Squared Off

Now that you know how, knit about 12 squares. Choose a bunch of colors. Use the same needles, same number of stitches, and same amount of rows for each square. Sew them together. Add fringe on each end, and you'll have a scarf to keep you warm on cold days.

11

Pile on the Pillows

Here's what you need

* 8 equal-sized knitted squares
* yarn needle
* **fiber fill**
* scissors

Here's what you do

1 With the yarn needle and tails from the squares, sew four squares together.

2 Sew the other four squares together.

3 Sew the edges of these two larger pieces together, leaving an opening about 3 inches wide for stuffing.

4 Stuff the pillow with fiber fill, then finish sewing up the pillow edge.

5 Add **tassels** to each corner (see page 13).

Tackling Tassels

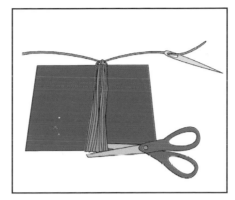

1 Wind yarn around a piece of cardboard about 8 inches wide.

2 Thread 12 inches of yarn onto a yarn needle. Pass it through the top of the yarn as shown. Tie tightly. Cut across the bottom of the looped yarn as shown.

3 Wind one of the tails tightly around the top of the tassel. Thread the yarn onto a needle and up through the top of the tassel. Use the tails to tie onto your project. Trim the ends of the tassel to make them even.

CHAPTER 4

Purl Marks the Spot

A bookmark is handy to have, and it makes a great gift too.

Learn how to make the purl stitch, and you've practically mastered the art of knitting. Making this bookmark will give you practice learning the purl stitch.

Knitting one row and purling the next creates a pattern called the **stockinette stitch**. The stockinette stitch looks like vertical rows of little tiny Vs.

Here's what you need

* knitting needles (small size, such as 2, 3, or 4)
* fingering weight yarn
* scissors
* yarn needle

Here's what you do

1 Cast on 12 stitches.

2 Row 1: Knit every stitch.

3 Row 2: Purl every stitch (see page 15).

4 Repeat steps 2 and 3 until the piece measures about 6 inches. Bind off all stitches.

5 With yarn needle, weave in yarn tails. Trim tail ends with scissors.

6 Add a piece of fringe to the top of the bookmark (see page 9).

Purl Stitch

1 With yarn in front of the work, slip the right needle into the stitch on the left needle going from right to left. The needle should be in front of the left needle.

2 Wrap the yarn over the right needle, around to back, and then to front as shown.

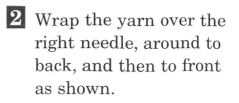

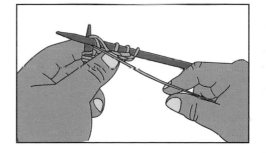

3 Use the tip of the right needle to pull the loop of yarn down through the stitch on the left needle.

4 Slip the left needle off the new purl stitch which is now on the right needle.

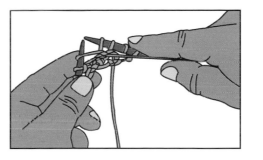

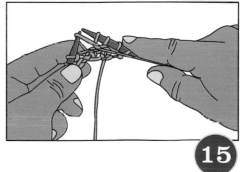

Getting your knits and purls mixed up? Use this handy chart to keep your stitches straight.

	Knit	Purl
needle position	right needle under left needle	right needle over left needle
direction through stitch	needle goes through left side of stitch	needle goes through right side of stitch
yarn position	always in back; wrap left to right	always in front; wrap right to left

CHAPTER 5

Use Your Head

A different combination of knit and purl stitches is called the ribbed stitch.

Knit one stitch, purl the next, and you've mastered the **ribbed stitch**. Use it to make a stylish headband.

Here's what you need

* knitting needles (medium size, such as 5, 6, or 7)
* yarn
* scissors
* yarn needle

Here's what you do

1 Cast on 12 stitches.

2 Row 1: Knit 1 stitch, purl 1 stitch. Repeat across row.

3 Repeat step 2 until piece is long enough to fit around your head.

4 Bind off all stitches.

5 With yarn needle, sew cast-on edge to bound-off edge.

Your ribbed stitch will look like this.

Magic Six Pincushion

Look what happens with one single purl stitch.

This fun pincushion calls for one single purl stitch every other row. Wait until you see what happens. The piece will have a natural fold line. Use different color yarn for each layer, or alternate between two colors. This project gets its name because most everything is connected with the number—you guessed it—six!

Here's what you do

1. Cast on 25 stitches. (Be patient, and you'll soon see how "six" fits in.)

2. Row 1: Knit 12 stitches, purl one stitch, knit 12 stitches.

3. Row 2: Knit 25 stitches.

4. Repeat rows 1 and 2 to make 12 rows total (6 **garter stitch** ridges).

5. Bind off all stitches.

6. Fold the piece in half (that one purl stitch will make it easy). Sew cast-on edge to bound-off edge. Set aside.

7. Repeat steps 1 through 3 until you have 24 rows total (12 garter stitch ridges). Bind off.

8. Fold this piece in half and wrap it around the first piece. Sew the cast-on edge to the bound-off edge.

9. Continue repeating steps 1 through 3 adding 12 rows (6 garter stitch ridges) each time.

10. When you are finished, your pincushion should have six rings. Did you notice that the number of knit stitches and the number of rows are all divisible by the number six? See why it's called the "Magic Six" Pincushion?

CHAPTER 7

I-Cords

What on earth is an I-Cord?

I-Cords are knitted tubelike strings. You can use them for so many projects, such as this fashionable I-Cord belt. You're going to need a pair of double-pointed needles. That's right—there's a point on both ends of the needles. But don't worry. It's not nearly as tricky as it sounds.

Here's what you need

* pair of double-pointed needles
* yarn
* scissors
* yarn needle

Here's what you do

1 Cast on 3 stitches.

2 Knit 3 stitches.

3 Slide stitches to other end of the needle.

4 Bring yarn around the back of the stitches, and knit three stitches again.

5 Continue until the I-Cord is the length you want. Then cut the yarn about 6 inches from the last stitches.

6 With a yarn needle, thread the end of the yarn through the stitches and pull securely.

Belt It Out

Add some style to any outfit with a cool belt. With bulky yarn and about six stitches, make an I-Cord the length of your waist plus 12 inches or more. Knot the cord at each end. Add some tassels for extra flair.

Carry Your Stuff with Style

Even more fun with I-Cords!

I-Cords are pretty strong, so they make great purse handles or ties for lots of projects. Now that you know how to make I-Cords, knitting this purse will be a snap. Start with two I-Cords. One should be about 3 inches long. The other should be about 20 inches long. Set them aside.

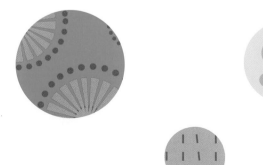

To Spool or Not to Spool?

Long ago, girls made I-Cords with an empty wooden spool. A few nails around the center hole held the yarn in place. The emerging I-Cord went down through the hole in the center of the spool. Most of these spools were homemade.

Today, many yarn shops sell knitting spools to make I-Cords. They come with instructions to help you get started. These newer versions of the knitting spool work on the same principle as the old-fashioned kind. If you just can't get the hang of the double-pointed needle method of making I-Cords, you may want to try a knitting spool.

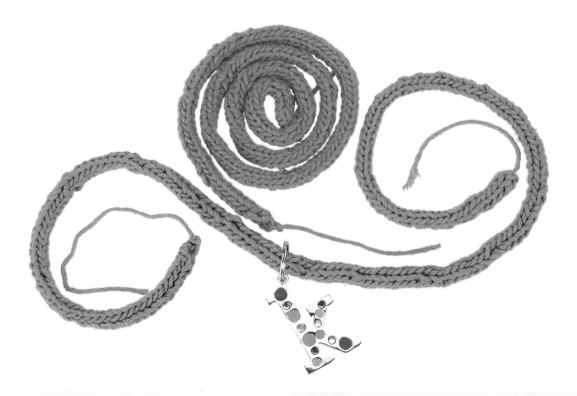

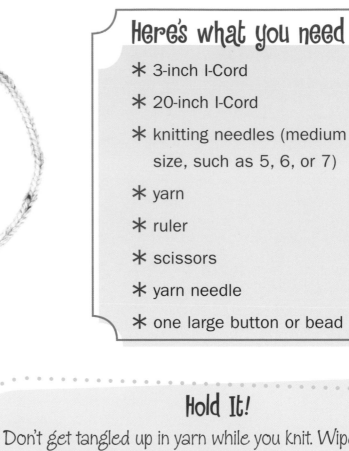

Here's what you need

* 3-inch I-Cord
* 20-inch I-Cord
* knitting needles (medium size, such as 5, 6, or 7)
* yarn
* ruler
* scissors
* yarn needle
* one large button or bead

Hold It!

Don't get tangled up in yarn while you knit. Wipe out an empty oatmeal box. Glue some fun paper around the outside of the box. Then poke a hole in the middle of the plastic lid and use scissors to make the hole smooth. Dab some clear nail polish inside the hole. This trick will keep your yarn from snagging. Finally, put your yarn inside the box and string the end of the yarn through the hole in the cover.

Here's what you do

1 Cast on 30 stitches.

2 Rows 1 through 10: Knit every stitch.

3 Row 11: Purl every stitch.

4 Row 12: Knit every stitch.

5 Repeat rows 11 and 12 until piece measures 9 inches.

6 Repeat rows 1 through 10. Bind off.

7 Fold the pieces in half and sew side seams.

8 Sew both ends of the 3-inch I-Cord to the middle top of one side of the purse.

9 Sew a large button or bead on the opposite side of the purse.

10 Sew ends of 20-inch I-Cord to sides of purse.

11 With yarn needle, weave in yarn tails. Trim tail ends with scissors.

Button Up!

Accessories change ordinary clothes into fashion statements. Buttons, for example, can really jazz up a sweater or a knitted purse. Because this knitted purse has a single button, it's important to select one that reflects your personality. Maybe a funky bead is what you need.
Or perhaps a big, colorful button suits you better.

CHAPTER 8

It's a Wrap

It's time to splurge on some crazy, funky yarn.

Now that you've practiced your knitting skills, it's time to show off what you can do. For these great scarves, find a wacky **skein** of really furry, curly, or fuzzy yarn. You'll also want a pair of really large knitting needles. The rest is easy.

Here's what you do

1 Cast on about 10 stitches (fewer for a narrower scarf, more for a wider scarf).

2 Knit every stitch in every row.

3 When scarf is the length you want, bind off all stitches.

4 With yarn needle, weave in yarn tails. Trim tail ends with scissors.

Fast Facts

Knitting for a Cause

During World War I (1914–1918), children in the United States knit to help the war effort. Friday afternoons in school, boys and girls knit squares that were later sewn into blankets. The colorful blankets were used in hospitals that treated injured soldiers.

A Whale of a Needle?

Long ago, knitting needles were made of baleen. Baleen is a tough, hornlike material that grows like fringe along the upper jaws of certain whales. Today, knitting needles are made of a variety of materials. Some are plastic or aluminum. Others are made of bamboo or decorative wood like rosewood, cherry, and ebony.

Sizing Up Your Needle

Not sure what size needle you have? You can find the size of any needle with a needle gauge. The smallest hole on the needle gauge that fits the widest part of your needle tells you its size.

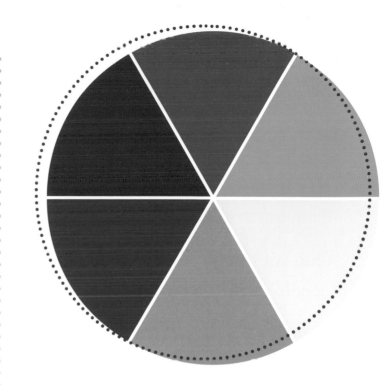

Color Wheel

Yarn comes in every color imaginable. How do you choose colors that work well together? Think of the color wheel. The colors next to each other work together in harmony. Colors opposite each other have a stronger effect when used together because they have more contrast.

Glossary

bind off (BINDE AWF)—to take stitches off the needle in a way that keeps them from unraveling

cast on (KAST ON)—to add stitches to a needle at the beginning of a project

drop a stitch—to accidentally allow a stitch to slip off the needle while knitting

fiber fill (FYE-bur FIL)—a material made of polyester fiber; fiber fill is used to stuff pillows.

garter stitch (GAR-tur STITCH)—a knitting pattern made by knitting every stitch in every row

purl (PURL)—a backward knit stitch

ribbed stitch (RIHBBD STITCH)—a knitting pattern made by alternating one knit stitch with one purl stitch

skein (SKAYN)—a loosely coiled length of yarn

stockinette stitch (STOCK-in-eht STITCH)—a knitting pattern made by alternating one row of knit stitches and one row of purl stitches

tassel (TASS-uhl)—a bunch of threads tied at one end and used to decorate pillows, furniture, and many other items

Read More

Blanchette, Peg. *Kids' Easy Knitting Projects.* Quick Starts for Kids! Charlotte, Vt.: Williamson, 2001.

Bradberry, Sarah. *Kids Knit!: Simple Steps to Nifty Projects.* New York: Sterling, 2004.

Wenger, Jennifer, Carol Abrams, and Maureen Lasher. *Teen Knitting Club.* New York: Artisan, 2004.

Internet Sites

FactHound offers a safe, fun way to find Internet sites related to this book. All of the sites on FactHound have been researched by our staff.

Here's how:

1. Visit *www.facthound.com*
2. Choose your grade level.
3. Type in this book ID **0736864733** for age-appropriate sites. You may also browse subjects by clicking on letters, or by clicking on pictures and words.
4. Click on the **Fetch It** button.

FactHound will fetch the best sites for you!

About the Author

Kay Melchisedech Olson was formerly the editor of *Workbasket* magazine as well as *Easy-Does-It Needlework and Crafts* magazine. She wrote a number of articles for children learning to knit.

Kay learned to knit with praise and by example from her grandmother, Myrtle Born. Grandma Born knit so many mittens for her children, grandchildren, and great-grandchildren that she earned the nickname Grandma Mitten.

Index